Six Presents from GOD

Sermons and Children's Object Lessons
for Advent and Christmas

GARY HOUSTON

C.S.S. Publishing Co., Inc.
Lima, Ohio

SIX PRESENTS FROM GOD

Library of Congress Cataloging-in-Publication Data

Houston, Gary W., 1943-
    Six presents from God.

    1. Advent sermons.   2. Christmas sermons.   3. Children's ser-
mons.   4. Methodist Church — Sermons.
5. United Methodist Church (U.S.) — Sermons.   6. Sermons, American.
I. Title.   II. Title: 6 presents from God.
BV40.H68   1988   252'.53   88-7260
ISBN 1-55673-072-1

8869 / ISBN 1-55673-072-1   PRINTED IN U.S.A.

Table of Contents

Foreword   5

Advent 1
"Angels" (Children's Sermon)   7
A Present of Angels   8

Advent 2
The Heart of Mary (Children's Sermon)   14
A Present of Mary   15

Advent 3
The Christmas Shepherd (Children's Sermon)   22
A Present of Shepherds   23

Advent 4
The Wisemen (Children's Sermon)   29
A Present of Wisemen   30

Christmas Eve/Day
The Baby Jesus (Children's Sermon)   36
A Present of the Baby Jesus   37

Christmas 1
Joseph (Children's Sermon)   43
A Present of Joseph   44

Acknowledgments   51

About the Author   52

Dedicated to the memory of the Reverend Harold W. Houston who died on Thanksgiving Day, 1987 after over thirty years of faithful ministry. Thank you, Dad.

Foreword

There are so many presents which we receive from God that we often fail to acknowledge some obvious ones. Besides our health, friends, family, jobs and so on we were also given six tremendous presents around 1988 years ago. These six were: *Angels, Mary, Shepherds, Wisemen, Jesus* and *Joseph.*

Angels symbolize various messages and messengers from God. They can remind us of Prophets (both Old and New Testament), John the Baptizer, and even good friends who point us on the right path. (Don't forget the angel on top of our Christmas trees!)

Mary symbolizes purity, holiness, warmth, and grace, and can be a wonderful example for mothers and grandmothers. Mary helps balance our intellectual beliefs with our heart's faith. One suggestion would be to decorate a tree with hearts. Who says hearts are reserved for Saint Valentine's Day?

The shepherds remind us of the humanity and humility of Jesus. Shepherds demonstrate concern for others. (We are all sheep, by the way. Jesus told us this. When we become lost the Great Shepherd is always seeking us.) Candy canes on the tree remind us of this gift.

The wisemen show us that all human wisdom bows down before God's majesty. They can remind us that the Old Testament law preceded New Testament grace. Also, they show us the grace of God's guidance when we follow his star. Stars, either white or of various colors, on the tree could remind us of this great present from God.

Jesus points us to grace, love, courage and faith. He can be represented by the lights on the Christmas tree. Jesus anchors us here on earth with his practical concern for others when our minds wax too mystical. We can be lights for others as we demonstrate Jesus by our very lives.

And, finally, *Joseph* represents faithfulness to God. He faithfully carried out the task God had given him helping to nuture the Christ child. Not only is Mary overlooked by Protestants, but Joseph is as well. Our Roman Catholic friends associate Joseph with healing and health. I would not personally represent Joseph on the Christmas tree. Instead, I would see him symbolized as we carry the tree out of the church (after Christmas). Joseph got the job done as he followed divine dreams. He is a good model for church work.

Please accept this little book of sermons as humble suggestions for your own sermons. It is doubtful that you will want merely to copy them. I hope you let them launch you into your own set of exciting Christmas sermons in your particular church setting. This has been a labor of love which I joyfully share with you. I want to thank my wife Joyce for typing it and my children Joshua and Denise for inspiring some of it.

1. Angels

A Children's Sermon

I asked you all to bring in an angel ornament today to put on our tree. And now I want to ask you to tell me what you think the main difference between an angel and a human might be? It's a pretty hard question isn't it?

Let's think together. Can we? Well, an angel can fly and a human can't. What else? Angels live in heaven, don't they? And we don't. Oh yes, angels sing better than we do. At least better than some of us do — like me.

But that's not what I was thinking about. Does anyone else have any ideas? *(Pause. The suggestions could be interesting.)* I think the main difference is that angels didn't have Jesus die for them. They didn't need him to do that. Because, you see, angels — at least the ones who live in heaven with God — have never sinned. Since they don't sin, then they don't need salvation from sin. But humans living on their own are in pretty bad shape without Jesus. In fact, they are lost.

This angel figure reminds me that I'm human. But that's neat, because it also makes Jesus more real for me. I hope it does for you. Remember that Christmas is all about God becoming human just like you and me.

Advent 1

A Present of Angels

Luke 1:5-25   *Advent 1*

Little Hugh had been fascinated about the sermon he had heard on angels. As he was telling a friend about it, they got into an argument. The little friend insisted that all angels had wings, but Hugh disagreed. "It isn't true," insisted Hugh. "Our preacher says that some of them are strangers in underwares."

How often have you given serious thought to the subject of angels? Perhaps never? Billy Graham writes in his book *Angels: God's Secret Agents,* "The empire of angels is as vast as God's creation. If you believe the Bible, you will believe in their ministry. They crisscross the Old and New Testaments, being mentioned directly or indirectly nearly 300 times. Some biblical scholars believe that angels can be numbered potentially in the millions since Hebrews 12:22 speaks of "an innumerable (myriads — a great but indefinite number) company of angels."[1]

What we would like to do this first Sunday of Advent is to focus for a few minutes on the topic "God's Present of Angels." We will find that not only were angels important during "Bible days," but they are in *our* days as well.

Did you know that the Bible teaches there are nine orders of angels? In *The Philokalia,* which is a collection of spiritual teachings of Eastern Orthodoxy, one early saint known as Peter of Damaskos, who lived around A.D. 1200, had this to say:

"Now I will say something about the contemplation of the angelic orders. According to Saint Dionysios the Aeropagite and as we find confirmed in Holy scripture (cf. Isaiah 6:2; Ezekiel 1:5; Romans 8:38; Ephesians 1:21; Colossians 1:16; 1 Thessalonians 4:16), there are nine such orders.

"These nine orders have been named according to their natures and activities. They are called 'bodiless' because they are non-material, 'spiritual' because they are intellects, and 'hosts' because thay are the ministering spirits of the King of all (cf. Luke 2:13; Hebrews 1:14). They also have other names and titles both specific and general; thus they are called 'powers' (cf. Ephesians 1:21; 1 Peter 3:22) and 'angels', that is to say 'messengers' (cf. Matt. 1:20).

" 'Powers' is the name of a single order but is applied also to all nine orders with regard to their activities for all have been empowered to fufill God's will. Again one particular order — that which is closest to us and ninth for God's inaccessible throne — is called the order of 'angels'; yet with regard to their activities all are called 'angels,' or 'messengers,' because all announce the divine ordinances to men."[2]

Saint Bonaventure mentions these nine orders when he quotes Bernard of Clairvaux: "God loves in the Seraphim as charity, knows in the Cherubim as truth, is seated in the Thrones as equity, reigns in the Dominations as majesty, rules in the Principalities as principle, guards in the Powers as salvation, acts in the Virtues as strength, reveals in the Archangels as light, assists in the Angels as piety."[3]

The seraphim, as we know from Revelation 4:8, Isaiah 6:2 and Ezekiel 1:6, are rather strange looking. They have many eyes and six wings and stay continually near the throne of God, offering praise.

The cherubim are similar to the seraphim, but we read in Isaiah 6:3 that the seraphim sing, "Holy, holy, holy is the Lord of Hosts." We do not read that the cherubim sing. These cherubim are first mentioned in Genesis 3:24, when God drove Adam and Eve from the Garden of Eden and placed cherubim at the east of the garden. The cherubim had a flaming sword which kept sinful humans from this divine paradise.

The other two ranks of angels about which we have any information in the Bible are (a) archangels and (b) what are simply called "angels." Michael is called an archangel in Jude 9. In the Old Testament Michael is identified with Israel. He is a type of guardian archangel, but he can fight with and will conquer Satan. Michael seems to be a favorite of God and probably stands as the general of heaven.

The term angel itself simply means "messenger." One of the more prominent of these is Gabriel, who serves as a special messenger of God. It was Gabriel who brought the news to Mary that she would bear the Christ child. It was also Gabriel who told Zacharias that John, later called "The Baptizer," would be born to his wife Elizabeth. Both times when Gabriel appears in Luke's Gospel it is to bring joyous news from God. Gabriel tells Mary:

Rejoice, highly favored one,
the Lord is with you;
blessed are you among women.

It was probably Gabriel who led the chorus of angels that appeared to the shepherds that night, for again the message is one of great news from God. The angel says:

Do not be afraid
for behold,
I bring you good tidings of great joy
which will be to all people.
For there is born to you this day
in the city of David
a Savior, who is Christ the Lord.
And this will be a sign to you:
You will find a Babe
wrapped in swaddling cloths,
lying in a manger.

What marvelous news Gabriel brought, straight from God's holy throne! The most monumental event in world history was soon to transpire and Mary and the shepherds received the news first-hand from an archangel.

Now Joseph received a heavenly messenger in another manner. An angel appeared to him in dreams — first with the warning to go to Egypt and then later with good news, telling him to return to Israel since Herod was dead. In this way we know that God was directly involved in this divine event. Angels set the stage for the birth of Jesus. His birth was announced by angels. And he was protected by angels.

This brings us, then, to another function of angels, namely that we are under the *protection* of God's angels. The notion of guardian angels has biblical support. In Matthew 18:10 Jesus tells his disciples, "Take heed that you do not despise one of these little ones, for I say to you that in heaven their angels always see the face of my Father who is in heaven."

Saint Peter of Damaskos believed that we all receive a guardian angel when we are baptized. Hear his words:

> First, we must recognize that the starting point of all our spiritual development is the natural knowledge given us by God, whether this comes through the Scriptures by human agency, or by means of the angel which is given in divine baptism to guard the soul of every believer, to act as his conscience and to remind him of the divine commandments of Christ. If the baptized person keeps these commandments, the grace of the Holy Spirit is preserved in him.[4]

Then again he writes: "God has done all things for our benefit. We are guarded and taught by the angels; we are tempted by the demons so that we may be humbled and have recourse to God, thus being saved from self-elation and delivered from negligence."[5]

The reason the angels protect us is that they are actively involved in the cosmic drama, fighting on our side against forces of evil. We are told that they rejoice over the salvation of every sinner. So they do not simply protect our bodies from harm from time to time. Instead, they fight continually to preserve the Gospel which Gabriel first proclaimed. "Jesus is born!" They are still interested that others hear that good news.

That great old Christian of the second and third centuries named Origen refused to speculate on how we are guarded. But he believed that we are. At one point in his work entitled "On Prayer," he said, "And even though we do not know exactly who the angel is assigned to each of us, who sees the Father's face in heaven (cf. Matthew 18:10), nevertheless it is evident upon consideration that we are debtors for certain things to him. And if we are in a theater of the world both of angels and of men, we must know that, just as the person in a theater is a debtor to say or do certain things in the view of the spectators and if he fails to do them is punished for having insulted the whole theater, so also we are debtors to the whole world, both to all the angels and to the human race, for those things we shall learn from Wisdom if we are willing."[6]

Paul reminds us in Ephesians 6:12 that our struggles are not only against flesh and blood, but that we are fighting against "principalities, against powers, against the rulers of the darkness of this age, against spiritual hosts of wickedness in heavenly places." There are good angels and there are bad angels. There are most likely millions of bad angels who followed Lucifer into rebellion against God. Revelation 12:7-9 tells us that these bad angels have deceived the whole world.

If this is true, and we believe it to be as our Bible teaches, then we must take angels seriously. We should thank God that angels will carry us to God's throne when we die. We need not fear the demons of the air because God's angels will carry us safely past.

Nor should we forget that some day Michael and the other angels, under Christ's leadership, will bind up Satan and cast him and all his followers into the Lake of Fire. Billy Graham asserts that he is an optimist because he has read the last page of the *New Testament*. And even there, we might add, there is talk of angels.

Let us thank God for his Gift of Angels!

1. Billy Graham, *Angels: God's Secret Agents*. (Waco: Word Books, revised 1986), p. 27.

2. Saint Peter of Damaskos, "Knowledge of the Angelic Orders," found in *The Philokalia*, vol. III, translated and edited by G.E.H. Palmer, Philip Sherrard, and Kallistos Ware, (London: Faber and Faber, 1986), pp. 250, 251.

3. *Bonaventure, The Soul's Journey Into God, The Tree of Life, The Life of St. Francis*, translated by Ewert Cousins, (New York; Paulist Press, 1978, The Classics of Western Spirituality Series), p. 90.

4. Saint Peter of Damaskos, "A Treasury of Divine Knowledge," found in The Philokalia, vol. III, p. 76.

5. Saint Peter of Damaskos, "How God Has Done All Things For Our Benefit," op. cit., p. 173.

6. Origen, "On Prayer," translated by Rowan A. Greer, found in *Origen: An Exhortation to Martyrdom Prayer*, (New York: Paulist Press, 1979, The Classics of Western Spirituality), p. 148.

2. The Heart of Mary

A Children's Sermon

Boys and girls, you have probably seen a heart like this before haven't you? On what other special day do we see hearts? It's in February. That's right, Valentine's Day! Did you ever hear of celebrating Valentine's Day around Christmas? Well this heart still reminds us of love — even at Christmas.

But we are also told, over and over in the New Testament, that Mary kept something about Jesus in her heart. Isn't that a wonderful place for Jesus to live? So this heart reminds us that Jesus lives in our hearts. And like Mary, his mother, we can show that we know Jesus loves a heart on our Christmas tree each year. That will remind us.

And do you know what else? When people see big red hearts on our Christmas tree, they'll be surprised. They will want to know what the hearts mean. At this time we can tell them all about Jesus, whom we love and worship.

When we think of Jesus' mommy we remember that she must have loved him just like our mommies love us. Isn't it wonderful to be loved? That's why we have hearts on our tree.

Advent 2

A Present of Mary

Luke 1:26-38   *Advent 2*

One person has written of the Virgin Mary:

> *The Mary of the New Testament represents all that was finest in Jewish womanhood and motherhood. Her deep spiritual sensitivity; her purity, faith, and obedience to the divine will; her scrupulous attention to the training of her son in the religious traditions of his people; her loyalty to him, as evidenced by her presence at the Cross, even when she did not fully understand him — all mark her as a person of remarkable qualities.*"[1]

Most Protestant Christians don't give Mary enough credit. Just think about it. Mary is an excellent model of humility and service to God, one we could well follow. We shall return to this point again and again.

There is a basic outline of Mary's activities in the New Testament, but we do not have as much material as we would wish. There is the Annunciation. (Luke 1:26-38) Next there are the childhood events of Jesus with his mother. (Matthew 1:18 — 2:23; Luke 1:26 — 2:52) Mary is present at the wedding at Cana. (John 2:1-12) She faithfully stands by the cross of her crucified son. (John 19:25-27) And, finally, we find her in union with the apostles between the time of the Ascension and Pentecost. (Acts 1:14)

I. *The Annunciation* refers to the announcement by the angel Gabriel to Mary that God had chosen her to bear a son to be called Jesus. Mary was young, innocent and a virgin, and she was chosen by God to bear his son, the Messiah of the world. What an *honor* she was given!

Gabriel greeted Mary with these words: "Hail, O favored one, the Lord is with you." Gabriel tells Mary clearly that she has found favor with God. Can you imagine being told this directly by a heavenly angel? But rather than simply being overwhelmed, Mary responds: "Behold, I am the handmaid of the Lord; let it be to me according to your word."

We can see the faith of Mary by her answer to Gabriel. This is what we were referring to earlier. Mary is a model of Christian spirituality for us. She represents the soft, warm feminine spirit that we so much need in a sometimes masculine, aggressive world. When you and I are wed to Christ as his church we are called to obey and follow God's voice as did Mary.

Mary knew that she had not yet consummated her marriage with Joseph, but she also knew the power of God and that with him nothing is impossible. The incarnation of the preexistent Christ was a miracle. Tertullian reminds us that the Christ took on part of Mary's body:

> *So he was born from the Virgin; as Son of God he needed no earthly father, but it was necessary for him to derive his manhood from an earthly source. Consequently, being divine spirit . . . he entered into the Virgin, as the angel of the annunciation foretold, and received his flesh from her. The birth was a real one; he was born from her and not, as the Gnostic valentinus alleged, simply through her, as if she were a mere channel through which he passed . . . Christ's humanity was in every respect genuine, and also complete; it included, as indispensible to man's constitution, a soul as well as a body — indeed, the assumption of a soul was necessary if man was to be saved. As a result, he was obligated to put up with the passiones humanas, such as hunger and thirst, tears, birth and death."*

So Mary confronts us with the mystery of the Incarnation of God in human flesh. Christ took on the very flesh of his mother and walked among us. Mary then was the vehicle God chose to become like one of us. Let us not forget to remember and love Mary's present of Jesus to us this Christmas.

Oh, that the gift of Mary would remind us of miraculous, faith-filled living! We so often do not know what God could really do in our lives because our faith falls far short of Mary's. Mary's faith stands exalted and is an apt symbol for the church. If God is viewed as masculine and the church as feminine then the spiritual marriage of faith can transpire. But this takes our willingness and openness to new directions shown by God. God is showing you and me new things this very Christmas season. We can remain alert and ready to serve like Mary.

II. *The childhood of Jesus* demonstrated many miracles of God. We read of the shepherds being visited by heavenly angels. We are told of the wisemen from the east following God's star. And we know that Herod tried to use these very same wisemen to find the Christ child and kill him. We remember that Joseph was warned by an angel in a dream to take Mary and the baby Jesus and flee to Egypt.

We also remember that both Simeon and the prophetess Anna spoke of greatness of the baby Jesús. And we recall the story that Jesus remained behind in the temple that one time when he was twelve. When Mary and Joseph returned they found him. Like a typical, loving mother, when Mary discovered her lost son she said to him, "Son, why have you treated us so? Behold, your father and I have been looking for you anxiously."

Then Jesus said to her: "Did you not know that I must be in my Father's house?" Gently Jesus corrected his mother by showing her that although Joseph acted as his earthly father, his real father was God. By these and other comments Mary must have realized that her son was growing up. We do not know what other conversations Mary might have had with her son. Don't you wish we did? The Bible tells us all we need to know, but it doesn't always tell us all we would like to know.

III. *The wedding at Cana* is presented to us in the Bible as another picture of Mary and Jesus. You might remember that when the wine gave out, Mary said to Jesus: "They have no wine." Notice now what Jesus responded: "O woman, what have you to do with me? My hour has not yet come." Here Jesus is presented to us as fully mature. And the term "woman" is the same term that he later uses on the Cross when he commends the care of Mary to the apostle John. Now Mary told the servants, "Do whatever he tells you."

We remember the rest of the story — Jesus changed water into wine and the incident had a happy ending. Again we see the themes of faith and servanthood. Mary teaches us to follow Jesus by doing whatever he says to us. Like Mary, we can follow in humility and glorify Jesus with our lives.

IV. *When Jesus was on the Cross* it was his mother and the disciple he loved standing near. And he said to Mary, "Woman, behold, your son!" Then he said to the disciple, "Behold, your mother!" And we read, "And from that hour the disciple took her to his own home."

Notice that Jesus shifted the grief of his mother over a dying son to the love of one still living. Jesus showed that although he respected his mother Mary, he remained faithful to the will of his heavenly Father. But Mary was faithful as well, because even here in all her grief she did not desert God.

Can we imagine ourselves for a moment in this situation? Here was Mary who only about thirty years before had given birth to this miraculous son. She remembered the messages of the angels. She remembered the time in the temple. She remembered the wedding at Cana. Undoubtedly she also had many memories of Jesus playing as a boy. His smiles; his tears — Mary remembered them all.

Now her son was being crucified. Imagine the shock she must have felt. But we have no reason to think that even with her heart pierced Mary ever lost her faith in God.

I remember once, when I was around eleven years old, I played Jesus on the Cross in a church summer camp program. My own mother sat out in the audience. When I looked at her and she looked at me we both soon realized what must have happened on the day of the Crucifixion. I remember my mother cried.

You mothers who are here today, imagine yourselves for a moment in Mary's place. But even here we do not read of any spiritual rebellion on Mary's part. Mary still had faith that God's will was somehow being worked out. Mary, the most noble of women, one especially blessed by God, stood at the cross believing God.

V. Finally, we remember *Mary between the Ascension and Pentecost.* Mary who was faithful even before her son's life began remained faithful to God also after the Ascension as well. Mary waited for a further word from God and this word came on the Day of Pentecost. Again Mary is a symbol for the faithful church. Mary knew how to wait for instructions from God. And, if the instructions came slowly, she knew how to wait and hold these things in her heart.

Mary considered herself the handmaiden of the Lord. And in Luke 1:46-56 we have one of the most beautiful of hymns, known by many as "The Magnificat." This hymn is appropriate especially here near the Christmas season. Let us hear its words as Mary spoke — or sang — them:

My soul magnifies the Lord,
And my spirit has rejoiced in God my
Savior.

For he has regarded the lowly state of
his maidservant;
For behold, henceforth all generations
will call me blessed.
For he who is mighty has done great
things for me.
And holy is his name.
And his mercy is on those who fear
him
From generation to generation.
He has shown strength with his arm;
He has scattered the proud in the
imagination of their hearts.
He has put down the mighty from their
thrones,
And exalted the lowly.
He has filled the hungry with good
things,
And the rich he has sent away empty.
He has helped his servant Israel,
In remembrance of his mercy,
As he spoke to our fathers,
To Abraham and to his seed forever."

Mary rejoiced not only because she was pregnant, but because she saw all of creation pregnant with hope. She saw that the Savior of the whole creation would soon be born from her womb. What an honor! Julian of Norwich has said: "So our Lady is our mother, in whom we are all enclosed and born of her in Christ, for she who is mother of our savior is mother of all who are saved in our savior."

1. "Mary Mother of Jesus," *The Interpreter's Dictionary of the Bible*, (Nashville: Abingdon Press, 1962), vol. 3, p. 293.

2. J.N.D. Kelly, *Early Christian Doctrines*, (New York: Harper & Row, 1960) p. 150.

3. *Julian of Norwich: Showings*, translated Edmund Colledge, O.S.A. and James Walsh, S.J., (New York: Paulist Press, The Classics of Western Spirituality, 1978), p. 292.

3. The Christmas Shepherd

A Children's Sermon

Now how many of you here have heard of the Christmas shepherd? You haven't? Well, the Christmas shepherd is easy to recognize because he carries a candy cane instead of a staff.

Yes, of course, I'm teasing. But doesn't a candy cane remind you of the kind of staff or pole that shepherds used to carry? I think it does and that's what we can remember when we hang candy canes on our tree this year. Candy canes remind us of shepherds.

Now we might not all know why a shepherd carried a staff. Does anyone here know? *(Wait for answers.)* That's right. The staff was used to pull back sheep that were straying away from the safety of the herd. The shepherd didn't use the staff to beat the naughty sheep. Instead he pulled them back home.

Jesus is like that, isn't he? That's why we can call Jesus the Christmas Shepherd. He was born on Christmas. Christmas celebrates his birthday. And he is the Great Shepherd — the Christmas Shepherd. Aren't you happy to know that? I hope that every Christmas for the rest of your life you remember that Jesus is the Christmas Shepherd who loves you and protects you.

Advent 3

A Present of Shepherds

Luke 2:8-20   **Advent 3**

Imagine the surprise that the shepherds from Palestine had that first Christmas night! Picture what it must have been like to be watching over a flock of sheep, on a night like any other night, and suddenly to have an angel appear! Not only did these shepherds hear and see a divine messenger, but this angel had a strange message.

The angel said to them:

Be not afraid; for, behold, I bring you good news of a great joy which will come to all the people; for to you is born this day in the city of David a Savior, who is Christ the Lord. And this will be a sign for you: you will find a babe wrapped in swaddling cloths and lying in a manger.

Now I don't know about you, but if an angel appeared to me, I would be *frightened*. It would seem unreal. I would probably think I was going crazy. I'm just like that with unknown things. So the shepherds most likely were startled the way you or I would be. There is simply nothing in being a shepherd that prepares you to see angels.

Shepherding was one of the major occupations in Palestine at this time. We know, for example, that Abraham, Isaac, Jacob and David were all shepherds. There was nothing disgraceful about being a shepherd. But it was not an exalted occupation. Isn't it strange that the shepherds were among the first to know of the birth of God's Son? After all, the angel could have appeared to a king or an important government or religious figure. Why then to shepherds? Today, let us focus upon (1) God in Christ as our Shepherd and (2) us as sheep.

(1) God seems to have an interest in shepherds. In fact, God has been traditionally the Shepherd of Israel, watching over his people like sheep. Consider the first verse of Psalm 80:

> *Give ear, O Shepherd of Israel,*
> *thou who leadest Joseph like a flock!*

Or consider these words from Ezekiel 34:11-20:

> *For thus says the Lord God: Behold, I, I myself will search for my sheep, and will seek them out. As a shepherd seeks out his flock when some of his sheep have been scattered abroad, so will I seek out my sheep; and I will rescue them from all places where they have been scattered on a day of clouds and thick darkness. And I will bring them out from the peoples, and gather them from the countries, and will bring them into their own land; and I will feed them on the mountains of Israel, by the fountains, and in all the inhabited places of the country. I will feed them with good pasture, and upon the mountain heights of Israel shall be their pasture; there they shall lie down in good grazing land, and on fat pasture they shall feed on the mountains of Israel. I myself will be the shepherd of my sheep, and I will make them lie down, says the Lord God. I will seek the lost, and I will bring back the strayed, and I will bind up the crippled, and I will strengthen the weak, and the fat and the strong I will watch over, I will feed them in justice.*

We Christians often become too sentimental and mushy and do not get the whole picture. To avoid that in this case we must hear the conclusion of the passage:

As for you, my flock, thus says the Lord God: Behold, I judge between sheep and sheep, rams and he-goats. Is it not enough for you to feed on good pasture, that you must tread down with your feet the rest of your pasture; and to drink of clear water, that you must foul the rest with your feet? And must my sheep eat what you have trodden with your feet, and drink what you foul with your feet?

The angel appeared that night to the shepherds because they were a symbol of what God is like. God was the shepherd of Israel and his Son is the shepherd of the New Israel, all Christians. The shepherd cares about and worries over his sheep. But a shepherd also must sometimes use judgment between good sheep and bad sheep. The problem with many of us is that we want all the guidance and help — the green pastures — while we fail to stay in line and expect to escape judgment. We want to skip the main course and get to the dessert.

There is a fascinating book by Phillip Keller entitled *A Shepherd Looks At Psalm 23*. In this book Keller speaks of a problem sheep he once had in his flock in Africa. He called this sheep by the name of "Mrs. Gad-about." This sheep would always want to climb the fence and try to find a way into another pasture. Mrs. Gad-about was never contented with things as they were. The pasture on the other side of the fence might be barren or brown, but this never stopped Mrs. Gad-about.

And, what's more, Mrs. Gad-about taught all her lambs to climb through fences as well. They followed her example and soon were as good at causing trouble to the shepherd as the mother was. Then it became even worse. Mrs. Gad-about next taught others in the flock to be malcontents. The flock became so unsettled that something had to be done. Hear Keller's words:

"It was a difficult decision to make, for I loved her in the same way I loved the rest. Her strength and beauty and

alertness were a delight to the eye. But one morning I took
the killing knife in hand and butchered her. Her career of
fence crawling was cut short. It was the only solution to the
dilemma."

We can be glad that we have Jesus as our shepherd instead
of stern Phillip Keller. Yes, we can even laugh about Mrs. Gad-
about. However, it is like someone has said: we all like to ooh
and oogle the baby Jesus in the manger, but we don't like the
grown up Christ who lays demands upon us.

In the same way we like to read the twenty-third Psalm and
remember the faithfulness of the Good Shepherd towards us
sheep. All the while, however, many of us do not heed his voice
when he calls us.

In that well-known passage in the tenth chapter of John,
we hear of the Good Shepherd. Jesus says here that he lays
down his life for us sheep. He promises that unlike a hired laborer
he will not desert us if wolves come up. But he also reminds
his sheep to obey his voice.

This has been a problem for people since the days of an-
cient Israel. Isaiah 53:6 tells us, "all we like sheep have gone
astray, we have turned every one to his own way, and the Lord
hath laid on him the inquity of us all."

We Christians, of course, believe that our sins have been
laid upon Jesus at Calvary. Let us not forget, though, that we
have a constant responsibility before us to remain faithful and
to heed the voice of the shepherd.

(2) When we think of ourselves as sheep we are reminded
that this is how Christ referred to us. He must have had a sense
of humor when he uscd this imagery. Here's why: I always
thought of sheep as gentle, soft woolly creatures. Have you seen
them this way? So I had a sentimental notion of Jesus as the
Great Shepherd and myself as part of the faithful flock. Then
I read Phillip Keller's book and found out how stupid sheep are.
I am no longer flattered.

Keller has taught me, for example, that if a lead sheep

is spooked (say, by a rabbit) and jumps, then all the sheep following will jump even without knowing why. Aren't we like that? Don't we jump in fear if someone else does? Don't we spread gossip that someone else tells us? Don't we buy things because others do? Don't we fight battles with imaginary enemies? Surely we are like sheep. Some have called this the herd instinct.

Keller also speaks about "Casting." It seems that a sheep can sometimes lie down on its side and somehow manage to flip over onto its back. When this happens the sheep cannot right itself and simply kicks out wildly at the air. The real problem is that gases build up inside of the sheep and, if the shepherd does not find the sheep in time, it will die lying there on its back kicking wildly.

Do you see what I mean about Jesus' sense of humor? He was not only calling us little, sweet, humble critters that sometimes stray, to whom God says "Naughty, Naughty." He was also telling us that without following him we are so dumb that we kick ourselves to death.

But there are also some positive things to be said about sheep. For example, they produce wool, which can be made into clothes to keep others warm. In addition, most sheep can be herded by a wise shepherd. I pray that you and I remain among the good sheep that not only hear our Shepherd's voice, but obey it as well.

If we turn back to the second chapter of Luke we find that God sent the angel to the shepherds that night as a symbolic gesture in order to show that from now on there would be with us a Great Shepherd. The angel brought good news of a great joy, news about this Great Shepherd who would be born a humble babe in a manger. Little did these shepherds from Palestine know what a gift this Great Shepherd would be! He would lay down his very life for his sheep. And all he would ask would be that we be faithful sheep and follow him. If we can stop jumping at rabbits and climbing fences looking for greener pastures we will be all right.

This Advent season remember this present from God the gift of the Shepherd. And, when he calls you, heed his voice. He will keep you safe. He will make us to lie down in green pastures and he will keep all the wolves away from destroying us — if only we will follow him. Remember the Great Shepherd and keep your legs firmly on the ground, where they belong.

1. Phillip Keller, *A Shepherd Looks at Psalm 23*, (Grand Rapids: Zondervan, 1970), p. 34.

4. The Wisemen

A Children's Sermon

Who is the wisest person that you have ever known? *(Let the children answer.)* My "wisest person" was my grandfather. He was a dairy farmer. Do you know what he could do? He could always tell when it was going to rain or when it was time to pick the corn. He knew when a cow was ready to give birth to a calf. He knew many things.

He also knew when I was hungry, or tired, or bored. Is your grandfather like that? I'll bet he is. But my grandfather could also tell things by looking at the stars. He told me you would never get lost if you could read the stars.

Many years ago some other wisemen knew about the stars. They followed one special star all the way to Bethlehem and found the baby Jesus there. When we put a star on top of our Christmas tree, we remember those wisemen. But it's okay to remember your grandfather at Christmas time, too.

Advent 4

A Present of Wisemen

Matthew 2:1-12   *Advent 4*

Did you know that the wisemen are only mentioned here in this Matthew text, and nowhere else in the Bible? Did you know that there were not necessarily three of them? Do you know where they came from? Let's talk a few minutes about the wisemen and see what we can learn.

First of all, the Greek word used here is *magoi*, which is the plural of *magos*. This word is defined in a Greek-English dictionary as "Persian . . . also Babylonian wise man and priest, who was expert in astrology, interpretation of dreams and various other secret arts." Indeed, these wisemen came to Palestine and declared that they had read in the stars concerning the birth of the Messianic King.

Now you may not find all this strange at first sight, but look more closely. Why would astrologers from Babylon be interested in the birth of a Jew, whether Messiah or not? And why is this story told? Is it to encourage us to read our daily horoscopes?

The word *magos* came down later as our word "magician," a deceiver. A magician is someone who creates an illusion, so that what the eye thinks it sees is not true. Perhaps we could say that Matthew was pointing to the truth of Christ as opposed to the illusions of this world. But yet there is more here.

We must not forget that these wisemen were led to Christ by a star or stars. In other words, their information — which came from divination — was correct. They were not sorcerers or deceivers, but instead men who could read the signs of the times and see God's hand in all things. It was something like a heavenly ballet of stars directed by God's mighty baton. It was the moment for Christ to be born and these wisemen were among the very first to know. They knew even before the shepherds.

They came, we are told by Matthew, to worship this King of the Jews. Once again, this is strange. If they were Persians then they had their own king and were most likely followers of Zoroaster. And now that we mention it, who was Zoroaster?

Zoroaster lived about three hundred years before Alexander the Great, somewhere in the seventh century B.C. Many have claimed that he was the first monotheist. (Others think Moses was.) Zoroaster taught resurrection of the body, the doctrine of heaven and hell, the future judgment of the world, the struggle between a Satan figure and the All-Good God, and many other doctrines similar to later Judaism and Christianity. Judaism was most likely influenced by Persian beliefs.

Many scholars say that Judaism simply borrowed (or "stole") many doctrines from Persian religion when the Jews were in the Babylonian captivity. Hear these strong words:

> About six hundred years before the Christian era, the Jews who were carried away as captives to Babylon were in constant contact with the Iranians. During the seventy years of their exile they borrowed from the Zoroastrian faith various doctrines such as the belief in the immortality of the soul, the resurrection of the body and future reward and punishment. "It is well known," says Max Muller, "that these doctrines were entirely, or almost entirely, absent from the oldest phase of religion among the Jews."

What does all this prove? It proves that the Jews and the Persians talked to each other about their belief in God. It is a fair guess that, if any "borrowing" took place, it went both ways. But all of this may have been in Matthew's mind when he wrote about the wisemen from the east. It is likely that Matthew saw the Christ event as much more important than what anyone had believed before, Jew or Persian.

The wisemen from the east symbolize the superiority of the Christ over all belief systems. The recognition of Christ as the King of the Jews by these foreigners showed that Christ was their king as well. In faith they followed the Advent star.

In other words, Christ is superior to all the wisdom of the east, astrology and all. Maybe today that message needs to ring clear again as much eastern philosophy (generally misunderstood) has been imported into the west.

I recently bought a magazine that I will not name (so as not to be sued) that literally made me ill. It spoke of workshops led by channels (a fancy name for spirit mediums), sensory deprivation chambers, mind altering machines, power crystals, Mexican trips with shamans and so on. One book was advertized for sale, whose author claimed to remember his last ten lifetimes!

Incredibly, one ad was for a sponsor-a-cow program. I'm serious! So were they. If you would send in $50 per month you could adopt a cow and it would not be killed after it had outlived its usefulness. The people who ran the milk farm (and who were probably laughing up their sleeve) were so-called Western Hindus. Strangely, a few pages later in the magazine was an ad to sponsor a child for $30 a month. In other words, a cow is worth more than a child! Our world is in trouble, friends.

I happen to have a doctorate in eastern religions and what I see every day is a mixed up bag of so-called eastern religion and some humanism being packaged and sold to gullible Americans. Instead of wisemen coming from the east to worship Christ, they are peddling instant nirvana and bliss without morals. Individualism is rampant and the acknowledgment of God's sovereignty rare! Self-knowledge is held up as the highest wisdom.

You might remember the story of Jesus talking with the woman from Samaria at the well. She believed Jesus to be a prophet and said to him, "Our fathers worshiped on this mountain, and you Jews say that in Jerusalem is the place where one ought to worship." Jesus said to her, "Woman, believe Me, the hour is coming when you will neither on this mountain, nor in Jerusalem, worship the Father. You worship what you do not know; we know what we worship, for salvation is of the Jews. But the hour is coming, and now is, when the true worshipers will worship the Father in spirit and truth; for the father is seeking such to worship him. God is Spirit, and those who worship him must worship in spirit and truth."

The wisemen who came to the cradle of the Christ child showed that his recognition as Lord and King was to be universal. Christ is king for all who acknowledge Him as Lord of their life. And the truth of Christ stands above all human wisdom — Persian, eastern, or otherwise. And he is the only channel or medium that we need.

1 Corinthians 3:18-19 speaks of our worldly wisdom. Hear these words:

> Let no one deceive hemself. If anyone among you seems to be wise in this age, let him become a fool that he may become wise. For the wisdom of this world is foolishness with God. For it is written, "He catches the wise in their own craftiness."

Symbolically the wisemen coming from the east are important for us in two ways. (1) They demonstrate the universality of Christ. In other words, he is not only King of the Jews, or King of the East; he is King over all who believe in him. (2) The wisemen symbolize that God's wisdom is far superior to the wisdom of this world. Only those who become fools for Christ can be guided by divine wisdom. The wisdom for Christians comes from God, not man!

Proverbs 9:10 states that "The fear of the Lord is the

beginning of wisdom, and the knowledge of the Holy One is understanding." Like the wisemen from the east, we lay our most precious gifts before the Christ. And we see that all that we give is nothing compared to what he gives back to us.

And what wisdom we have does not come from studying the stars or chasing eastern gurus. Instead, it comes from self-less service to the King of all. For it is in giving that we receive. As we ponder the presents we will receive this Christmas, let us realize that one of them can be to have our life directed by the One who made those stars that the wisemen studied so many years ago. If you do not know Jesus as your King and Lord, go back and read once more about his birth, his death and his resurrection this Christmas.

There are two more things to be said about the wisemen. We do not know that there were really three of them. There might have been more. There were three kinds of gifts, but not necessarily three wisemen. Nor were these wisemen kings. (Read Matthew again!) The tradition that the three wisemen were kings began in the middle ages.

What is important to us is the symbolism that the story of the wisemen demonstrates. As we have seen, this story shows the universal kingship of Christ and the limits of human wisdom — wisdom when judged against God's wisdom.

The wisemen saw the star of Christ and they came to worship him. Oh, that others would also see that star this holy season! The star of Christ, the Advent star, breaks forth with hope into the bleak skies of our lives. Like a beacon from the very throne of God the star of Christ lights the entire world. The child that was born that holy night was "the true Light which gives light to every man who comes into the world." (John 1:9)

The Scriptures tell us "the star which they had seen in the East went before them, till it came and stood over where the young child was. When they saw the star, they rejoiced with exceedingly great joy." Don't you feel that joy this

Advent season?

The wisemen came to see him who was born King of the Jews. (Matthew 2:2) Little did they know that the same title would be above Christ's head on the cross: Jesus of Nazareth, The King of the Jews. The Gospel of John (19: 20-22) says that when Jesus was crucified and this sign was put above his head many people complained. They wanted the sign to say *"He said, 'I am King of the Jews.' "* Pilate replied, "What I have written, I have written."

There is a finality about Christ, isn't there? He demands absolute kingship over our lives and over our hearts. What about you? Have you seen his star? Do you call him your King, just as those wisemen were wise enough to do?

1. William F. Arndt and F. Wilbur Gingrich, *A Greek-English Lexicon of the New Testament* (Chicago: The University of Chicago Press, 1957), p. 486.

2. Rustom Masani, *Zoroastrianism: The Religion of The Good Life,* (New York; The MacMillian Company, 1971), pp. 18,19.

5. The Baby Jesus

A Children's Sermon

If you wanted to put something on or under the Christmas tree to remind you of the baby Jesus, what would you use? Some of you might have a baby brother or sister. Could we just put them here under the tree for a week or two?

Well, we could use a doll. We could either put a doll under the tree, or we could put a special baby ornament on the tree. But I have another suggestion. Why don't we let all the pretty electric lights remind us of the baby Jesus.

I think we can, and here's why. We know that the wisemen followed a star, or light from heaven. So if God used a light to point to his new-born Son, why can't we? We can! And later, when you are all grown up, you will read a book in the Bible called the Gospel of John. There you will read that Jesus is the "Light of the World."

Jesus is a bright light to follow. He will keep you from darkness and fear. When you are all alone and it's dark, just look at a light and think of the baby Jesus. Can you do that?

Christmas Eve/Day

A Present of the Baby Jesus

Luke 2:15-21   *Christmas Eve/Day*

Have you ever asked yourself what is really important about the baby Jesus? Why was God's Son to begin his mission here on earth *as a baby?* He was, after all, in the beginning before all things. Jesus could have come to earth as a fully-grown man.

In fact, the Gospel of Mark and the Gospel of John do not mention the birth of Jesus at all. Is this because they consider the birth unimportant? No. they simply wanted to address other issues about the one called Jesus. Mark wanted to stress the human teacher and John wanted to emphasize his divine nature.

Luke is the Gospel writer most concerned with the birth of Jesus. Luke depicts Jesus as the new baby lying in a manger. A manger, by the way, was a food trough for animals. It is strange that the Bread of Heaven humbled himself to be born in a manger. But that seems to be the way God works. He does the unexpected.

It is also highly symbolic that Luke tells us "there was no room for them in the inn." Visualize for a moment a cozy inn, perhaps with a warm fire, good food and wine. But the very Son of God could not be included in the hospitality of men and women. Instead, he began his life on this earth among animals, his parents and shepherds. What a humble way to begin a mission from eternity!

All of us have been babies, but we cannot remember what it was like to be so little, dependent and fragile. Look around at the babies present here today. Certainly they are cute and precious. But how much power do they have?

What do we mean by power? Well, a baby is rather helpless,

isn't it? I mean to say that parents have to take care of a baby, feed it, change it. Without parents of some kind, the baby would die. A baby needs power from others in order to survive.

There is reason to believe that the Son of God came as one who was small, fragile, and born outside the inn for a purpose. I believe the Christ was identifying with us. Humans are vulnerable and fragile. We are easily hurt. We are all rather helpless in many ways and many times we feel isolated and alone.

God sent the Son into the world in the same way you and I came into the world — as a baby! Jesus could have arrived fully-grown. He could have come to the earth in the form of an angel surrounded by glorious divine light. But he came as a small baby.

This baby identified with our struggles and temptations. He came to appreciate our plight. Jesus knows what you and I are going through. Jesus did not come to earth as a divine being disguised as a man. He was fully human. But he was fully divine as well. What an eternal mystery that is.

Our problem is not that most of us do not accept the divinity of Jesus. We do! It's his *humanity* that many find hard to accept. We do not want Jesus to be like us. We want him divine — all the time and all the way. If we think this way, however, we make Jesus too remote from us (when all the while he wants to be close to us). Jesus can be a friend because he understands us.

Jesus was born like us — as a baby. Once and for all he was born and placed in a manger, out with the animals. Are we still pushing him out of the inn? Are we pushing Jesus away when all the while he wants to be close to us?

John Gleason wrote a marvelous book that should be recommended to all Christians. It is entitled *Growing Up to God*, and in it Gleason says:

Jesus the adult had the physical features of his Semitic forebears — dark hair, eyes, and skin. Probably small in height by current standards, he had calloused carpenter's hands, sun-darkened face, and sand-hardened feet. Of considerable intelligence, Jesus had sharpened his mental capability by serious study of Scripture and of human nature, and had accordingly become sensitive to the needs of individuals and his nation as a whole.

In late adolescence and beyond, there was in his consciousness a growing sense of some important purpose for his life which increasingly became tied to the expectations of the nation for a Messiah, a God-sent leader who would deliver Israel from her oppressors and bring in a golden age. The usual sexual longings, family loyalties, and vocational goals were sublimated to the rising sense of calling and the ever-sharpening understanding of his role, though not without considerable inner turmoil and resistance.[1]

Can you and I allow God to send his Son in the form of a little, fragile baby? Can we allow this Jesus to grow up like us and face the same kinds of struggles we have faced? When I ask "Can we allow it?" I really mean to ask, "Can we *believe* it?" If we *can,* then we do not have a remote, strong, aggressive God who violated our freedom.

Instead we have a Lord who speaks to us in nudges, whispers and situations. You may be in a particular situation, or difficulty into which God has allowed you to come. Clearly God allows us to be humbled by adversities in order to correct our pride of self-sufficiency.

Bishop Fulton J. Sheen relates an incident that came from Plutarch. "Plutarch tells the story of a man who attempted to make a dead body stand upright. He tried various schemes of balancing, experimented with different postures. Finally he gave up, saying, 'There is something missing on the inside.' " Sheen concludes: "This is the story of Everyman."[2]

You and I are not self-sufficient. Inside us we can have the Holy Spirit of God, that which can animate us and make us more than animals. It was this inner communion, this "divine inside," — that made Jesus someone special. And as we allow God to empower us, to give us "in-spirit-action," then we become more and more like his Son Jesus.

If Jesus could be humble, fragile, vunerable, dependent and tempted, then what makes us think we have the right to escape these things? You and I need to reclaim our humanity. We are not beasts living for pleasure. We are humans. And humans have something special on the inside if they are Christians. We can and should be holy.

Harold Kohn in his book *Small Wonders,* provides an interesting illustration:[3]

> *If the earth were reduced to a diameter the size of the period at the end of this sentence, that is to say about one-fiftieth of an inch in diameter, and everything else in the universe were diminished in proportion, even then the known universe would be immense. With all astronomical distances shrunk to that microscopic scale, the astronomers estimate that the sun would be nineteen and one half feet away from the period-sized earth. The nearest star beyond the sun would be slightly more than one-thousand miles from the earth, and the farthest galaxy of stars would be nearly eighty-two billion miles away. So immense is the known universe this December. And so big was the world that long-ago night when the small Son of God split time with his sharp little birth cry, dropping the centuries into little heaps of B.C. and A.D.*[3]

Who says great things can't come in small packages? Any of you women who have ever received a gift of a diamond ring or earrings knows that the size of the Christmas package does not give it its value. Every great idea has a small beginning.

We need this Christmas to rediscover what the birth of Jesus as a baby really means to us. If we wish, we can see a three-fold scheme to the life of Jesus:

(1) His birth was a "sign of hope fulfilled." He was the Messiah of the Jews and the Savior of the world. This relates to the *past*. It has been done.

(2) His death was a "sign of deliverance." This relates to the *present* because each person can make a decision to accept this deliverance in the here-and-now. *Now* is the acceptable time for salvation. *Now* is the time to accept Jesus Christ as Lord of your life, and to let him fill your inside and make you fully human.

(3) His resurrection was a "sign of freedom from fear." This relates to the *future*. This is so not only because each of us will be resurrected on Judgment Day, but because once we are resurrected in our hearts we have love there instead of fear. The resurrected Christian steps bravely on through life — humbly, led by God.

Edward Bauman relates that Martin Niemoeller, who had been in a Nazi concentration camp, came to the United States after World War II. Reporters followed him around, expecting to hear him complain about his past difficulties. But they were disappointed. One reporter finally said: "All that man talks about is Jesus Christ!"[4]

Neimoeller did it because it is such a *joy* to speak of Jesus Christ. Jesus began as a baby in Bethlehem. In his growing he gave us three signs: (1) a sign of hope, fulfilled in his birth; (2) a sign of deliverance, announced in his death on the cross; and (3) a sign of freedom from fear, trumpeted in his resurrection. May you all be blessed in your shared humanity with Jesus. And may you have a new beginning this Christmas season!

1. John J. Gleason, *Growing Up to God* (Nashville: Abingdon Press, 1975), p. 94.

2. Fulton J. Sheen, *Peace of Soul* (New York: McGraw-Hill, 1949), p. 34.

3. Harold Kohn, *Small Wonders* (Nashville: Tidings, 1969), p. 11.

4. Edward W. Bauman *The Life and Teaching of Jesus*, (Philadelphia: The Westminster Press, 1960), p. 57.

6. Joseph

A Children's Sermon

If you children could pick anyone you wanted as your daddy, whom would you pick? Have you ever thought about that? I mean, if you could choose *anyone* in the whole world! Would you choose someone rich? Or would you pick someone you know would love you?

Jesus had his choice of any human daddy he wanted. Of course, Jesus wanted what his Heavenly Father wanted. But when he came to earth, Joseph was chosen to be his foster dad.

How many of you know what a foster dad is? It's not the same thing as a step-dad, is it? Well, a foster dad is someone who loves you enough to take care of you, feed you and buy you clothes and presents. But he is not your physical dad.

Joseph was a foster dad to Jesus. Joseph loved Jesus in a special way, and cared for him as he grew up. Joseph probably even taught Jesus how to build things. A person who builds things from wood is called a carpenter. Joseph was a carpenter and I'm sure he taught Jesus how to build all kinds of things.

We don't know for sure, but Joseph probably even taught Jesus how to read the Bible. We know that *someone* did, because Jesus knew the Psalms and the book of Isaiah well. Does your dad read the Bible to you? Maybe he would if you asked him.

You and I can be happy for daddys, can't we? We can show them, by the way we grow up and live, how much we appreciate the love they have given us. I hope your daddy is neat, like Joseph was. I'll bet he is.

Christmas 1

A Present of Joseph

Matthew 1:18-25   **Christmas 1**

How many of you here have known a young girl who got pregnant before she was married? I have seen this happen several times. It is worse in small towns where gossip freely flows. But some of us love to gossip about the misfortune of others, don't we?

In an excellent sermon entitled "That Naughtiness in Nazareth," Donald Brower captures well the flair of that event as he imagines the following conversation:[1]

> *Wait 'till I tell you what I heard in Nazareth! You know that young girl, Mary, the one who's betrothed to the carpenter Joseph? Well, I found out that she's got a cake in the oven. No, not that kind of cake; she's PG. I mean she's pregnant, for goodness' sake; she is going to have a baby. A kid yet, and the wedding isn't even scheduled for five more months. Oh, my gosh, the scandal. I'll bet her parents are mortified. I don't know what I'd do if something like that happened to my Gloria. And him a businessman and all that. I don't know if they're going to hurry up the wedding or what. Not much use in covering up what the whole town knows. I heard that Joseph told a friend of his that it wasn't his child, but whose would it be? Her folks keep pretty close tabs on her, and*

she hasn't been with anyone else. Joseph probably just doesn't want to admit it. Honestly, I don't know what young people are coming to today. This would never have happened when I was young. Why the next thing you know, these young girls will be telling their parents they don't want to marry the men their folks have contracted them to.[1]

Have you ever wondered what good, old, faithful Joseph must have thought? Matthew 1:19 says that "Joseph her husband, being a just man, and not wanting to make her a public example was minded to put her away secretly."

We need to remember that Joseph and Mary were not actually married yet. According to Jewish law, a man and a woman were betrothed for a period of one year before they were officially married. Only then was the marriage consummated. The couple did not have the sexual and property rights of husband and wife through this betrothal period. But if they wished to call off their approaching marriage during this period, the step was still called "getting a divorce."

It was during this year of betrothal that Joseph discovered that his soon-to-be wife was pregnant. This must have seemed a shock to a devout Jewish man. He was of the mind to handle this quietly and call off the marriage.

Perhaps the men in this congregation might want to put themselves in Joseph's place for a moment. What would *you* think if the woman to whom you were engaged was with child and you knew it wasn't yours?

Joseph did something strange, something that most of us would not have done. He changed his mind about divorcing her. He did it because of a dream. In this dream an angel appeared to Joseph and said:

Joseph, son of David, do not fear to take Mary as your wife, for that which is conceived in her is of the Holy Spirit; she will bear a Son, and you shall call his name Jesus, for he will save his people from their sins.

That was some message, wasn't it? Talk about a powerful dream! Imagine an angel appearing to you in a dream and telling you that your soon-to-be wife has conceived without a human father. And, what is more, her son will save people from their sins? It would be hard to go back to sleep again, wouldn't it?

Joseph could have ignored this dream. He could have written it off as indigestion or temporary insanity. Freud would have called it "wish fulfillment." In other words, Freud would have said that, since Joseph wanted to obtain Mary as his wife anyway, his subconscious merely tricked him into this dream.

There are several ways that God sends messages to us. Moses, you might remember, heard a distinct, external voice. But what is more common is to hear God through a dream, a strong intuition, a hunch, an external situation that strangely comes about.

Actually, I believe God is still guiding us today. We need only take the time, and have the awareness, necessary to see and hear it.

Our challenge is to become more consciously aware of the God within. It is not that the voice of God is not there. It is rather that we do not know how to listen.

Many wise people in many different cultures have learned to remember and pay attention to their dreams. So-called "primitive peoples" are often guided to fishing and hunting spots by their dreams. The aboriginal people of Australia, the Indians of North and South America, island peoples — many consider their dreams very carefully.

You might remember the dreams of another Joseph, visions recounted in Genesis 37. Joseph had a dream of the sheaves of his brother bowing down to his sheaf. A second dream told him that the sun, moon and eleven stars bowed down to him. His brothers were jealous and hateful toward him, but the dreams came true anyway. As a result, he rose to be the main assistant of the Pharoah in Egypt. God did something unexpected and new, both with this Joseph and with the one who become Jesus' foster dad as well.

In the tenth chapter of Acts we read that Peter went up on a rooftop to pray. There he fell into a trance. (We could as well say he fell asleep and dreamed.) He saw a great sheet let down from heaven. There were all kinds of creeping animals in it. A voice said to him, "Rise, Peter; kill and eat." Peter did not want to eat animals that the Jews considered unclean. But God was doing something new here. For the Christian there was not to be any distinction between clean and unclean animals.

We also might recall the "vision in the night" that Paul had. "A man of Macedonia stood and pleaded with him, saying, 'Come over to Macedonia and help us.' " And with this new information from God, received by the apostle through a dream, Paul's ministry was expanded.

I remember mentioning God's voice coming to us through dreams a few years ago in another congregation I once served. People would come up to me and smile strangely as if to say: "You poor, foolish boy, believing in dreams that way."

I am not saying that every dream is from God. Many dreams are from the level of the personal unconscious. Here the dreams appear as bizarre mixtures of memories, repressed wishes, and confusing symbols. Dreams from the personal unconscious seem to be similar to the visions that a schizophrenic sees. These dreams are crazy, mixed up and strange.

Dreams that arise from the collective unconscious, on the other hand, are powerful in symbolic content. These types of dreams are what Carl Jung, the noted psychiatrist called "big dreams."[2] These dreams are the ones to which "primitive people," shamans, and mystics pay attention. Big dreams occur especially when we are in periods of change — adolescence, mid-life, and facing death. Big dreams come from a deeper level of the unconscious than "little dreams" (ordinary dreams).

In his dreams, Joseph saw an angel. And the message from this angel was direct and clear. It was not a muddy, confused mess like most of our dreams are. When Joseph awoke from his sleep, he did as the Lord had commanded him. He took Mary to be his wife, but he did not have sexual relations with her until she had borne the son called Jesus.

In Matthew 2:13 we read:

> Now when they had departed, behold, an angel of the Lord appeared to Joseph in a dream, saying, "Arise, take the young child and His mother, flee to Egypt, and stay there until I bring you word, for Herod will seek the young Child to destroy him."

So Joseph and Mary fled with the infant to Egypt in response to a message from God in a dream.

> But when Herod was dead, behold, an angel of the Lord appeared in a dream to Joseph in Egypt, saying, "Arise, take the young Child and his mother, and go to the land of Israel, for those who sought the young Child's life are dead." Then he arose, took the young Child and His mother, and came into the land of Israel. (Matthew 2:19ff)

Again Joseph responded to the message of God through a dream.

Joseph knew his dreams and considered them important. His attention to his dreams changed his life course. Carl Jung placed importance on dreams, as the title of his autobiography *Memories, Dreams, Reflections* indicates. I have personally had several dreams which were prognostic in nature (they came true).

Many people have said to me that they never dream. This is simply not true. What is true is that they do not *remember* their dreams. John Sanford *writes:*

> One of the most interesting experiments with sleep was recently conducted by Dr. William Dement, while he was a research fellow in psychiatry at Mount Sinai Hospital in New York City. It can now be scientifically established whether and when a man is dreaming. This can be done first because of

*certain movements of the eyeball under the closed eyelid,
which the trained physician is able to detect, and secondly
because during dreams there is a change in the brain waves
of the sleeping person detectable by electroencephalogram.
With the aid of the electroencephalogram, experimenters are
able to waken a person in the middle of a dream. Several
experiments have revealed that all people dream on the aver-
age of about one-and-one-half hours per eight hours of sleep,
in about six or seven different dreams during the night. The
person who says he does not dream simply does not remember his dreams upon awakening.*[3]

Joseph, then, was a man who could be led by God. Joseph represented faithfulness and patience in the face of adversity. You and I, on the other hand, have a tendency to want to control everything that happens to us by the force of our wills. As we seek to guide our lives by conscious control and cease to rely upon God working through vehicles such as dreams, we often find only despair, pessimism and depression.[4]

Joseph had the courage to listen to the inner voice. This inner voice has been planted inside us by the God who is over all creation. The very power that moves planets is quite capable of guiding our actions.

It is not that God no longer speaks. In our busy and noisy world it is hard to pause and notice a dream or consider a hunch. Yet that is how God often works — softly and from within.

Joseph has too often been pushed out of Christmas. We prefer the dramatic twinkling stars of wisemen and the appearance of angels to shepherds. This Christmas season, let us not forget God's present of Joseph and the willingness of Joseph to follow a dream, wherever it might lead.

May you, too, have the courage to follow your dreams.

1. Donald Rings Brewer, "The Naughtiness In Nazareth," sermon published in Insights by J.L.J. Publishers, Springfield, Ohio, December, 1986.

2. Cp. C.G. Jung, *Dreams*, translated by R.F.C. Hill (Princeton: Princeton University Press, 1974), pp. 76-79.

3. John Sanford, *Dreams: God's Forgotten Language* (Philadelphia: J.B. Lippincott Company, 1968), p. 120.

4. See John Sanford, *op. cit.*, p. 124.

Acknowledgements

Publishers have granted the author permission to quote from the following materials:

Angels: God's Secret Agents by Billy Graham, 1986 Word Books. Used by permission.

The Philokalia, compiled by Saint Nikodimos of the Holy Mountain and Saint Makarios of Corinth, volume 3, 1984 Faber and Faber. Used by permission.

Bonaventure: The Soul's Journey Into God, The Tree of Life of Saint Francis, translated by Ewert Cousins, 1978 Paulist Press. Used by permission.

Origen: An Exhortation to Martydom, Prayer and Selected Works, translated by Rowan A. Greer, 1979 Paulist Press. Used by permission.

"The Naughtiness In Nazareth" by Donald Rings Brewer December 1986 *Insights*. From *Insights* Into Preaching, published by jlj publishers, Springfield, Ohio, December 1986. Used by permission.

A Shepherd Looks At Psalm 23 by Phillip Keller © W. Phillip Keller. Used by permission of Zondervan Publishing House.

A Greek-English Lexicon of the New Testament by William F. Arndt and F. Wilbur Gingrich, 1957 The University of Chicago Press. Used by permission.

About the Author

Gary W. Houston is a United Methodist clergy person presently serving Alexandria, Indiana First United Methodist Church. He has a Ph.D. in Inner Asian Studies (Indiana University, 1976) and graduated from an Episcopal seminary in Sewanee, Tennessee. He has authored/edited five published books and is a frequent contributor to *Emphasis, A Preaching Journal for the Parish Pastor.*